SCHOLASTIC

Grades
5 & Up

TIC-TAC-MATH

50 Reproducible, Leveled Game Sheets That Kids Can Use Independently or in Small Groups to Practice Important Math Skills

by Laura Meiselman

NEW YORK • TORONTO • LONDON • AUCKLAND • SYDNEY
MEXICO CITY • NEW DELHI • HONG KONG • BUENOS AIRES

Teaching *Resources*

*This book is dedicated to my favorite
daughter, Sophia Patterson.
May she love math half
as much as I love her.*

Cover design by Jaime Lucero
Interior design by Grafica, Inc.
Illustrations by Mike Moran

ISBN 0-439-62921-7

Table of Contents

Table of Contents

Introduction

Welcome to *Tic-Tac-Math: Grades 5 and Up!*
Your students are about to experience a wonderfully educational twist on one of the most popular games of all time. After all, what better way to grab students' interest than to announce, "Today, we're going to play a game!"

Just like classic tic-tac-toe, *Tic-Tac-Math* is played on a three-by-three grid that students mark with X's and O's to make a win. But unlike the traditional game, each square in the grid contains a math problem that students have to solve correctly before they can claim the square with their X or O.

What's Inside

Inside this book, you'll find 50 *Tic-Tac-Math* grids. Each grid covers a specific math skill that is tied to at least one of the NCTM (National Council for Teachers of Mathematics) standards. There are four sections that address the main standards: Number & Operations, Algebra, Data Analysis & Probability, Measurement and Geometry (we combined these last two standards into one section). The last section in this book offers a mixed review of different skills.

The problems within each grid are leveled so that problems on the top row are fairly easy, while the ones on the bottom row pose more of a challenge. Since the problems are leveled, you can decide which row (or column or diagonal, if you want students to try a variety of difficulty levels) will benefit each student the most. This way, every student can be working on the same topic but at his or her own level. (Make photocopies of the blank grid on page 8 to use as answer sheets for students or to create your own Tic-Tac-Math problems.)

Keep in mind that the point of each game is for students to practice and succeed at that particular math skill. By the time students have completed every grid in the book, they will have reviewed most of the math skills covered from grade 5 up to middle school. With those skills under their command, students will feel confident with the problems presented on standardized tests.

How to Use This Book

Tic-Tac-Math is a great way to reinforce a current math lesson or review a topic. Since each page focuses on a particular math topic, simply photocopy the page that corresponds with your unit of study and distribute to students.

Students can play *Tic-Tac-Math* with a partner, in small groups, or individually. Partners can play following the conventional rules of the game. Consider these additional rules as well:

- Flip a coin to decide who goes first, and who will be X and who will be O.

- If a player solves a problem correctly, that player marks the space with his or her letter (X or O).

- If the player answers incorrectly, the other player gets to mark that space with his or her letter *unless* that space would give the first player Tic-Tac-Math. (Players must correctly complete three problems in a row horizontally, vertically, or diagonally to get Tic-Tac-Math.)

- To win, a player must successfully solve the problem on the winning game space.

- Remind players to check each other's work!

Here are a few more ideas for using *Tic-Tac-Math:*

- **As a daily warm-up:** Have students complete three problems as a warm-up at the start of the class. Doing problems when students first enter the classroom helps them get settled and ready to work.

- **For "fast finishers":** Make sure to have some grids available to give students as a "What to Do When You're Done" activity.

- **For homework:** Send home a sheet for students to practice a particular skill. If you are working on adding fractions, for example, you can pass out a grid and assign students to complete any three problems—vertically, horizontally, or diagonally. Encourage students to play the game with parents or siblings.

- **As a choice activity:** Offer Tic-Tac-Math as a fun activity for choice time. Consider copying the grids onto cardstock and even laminating them so you can reuse them. Students can use different-colored counters instead of marking the grids with their X's and O's. Store the grids in a labeled folder or envelope for easy access. If you are using several different grids during one game session, encourage students to rotate around the room and play with as many other students as possible. Students gain a great deal from learning how to work with those to whom they might not normally gravitate toward in class.

Whichever approach you decide to use, your students are sure to enjoy themselves as they build the skills they need to succeed in math and on standardized tests. Let the games begin!

Name(s): _____

Name(s): _____

Let's Have "Sum" Fun!

Sum up three addition problems to get Tic-Tac-Math!

7,532 + 3,269	18,475 + 3,941	38,238 + 37,882
741,508 + 20,676	89,429 + 65,752	3,813,455 + 794,567
May DeSplash surfed on 11,832 waves one summer, and 34,729 the next summer. How many waves did she surf on in both summers?	Sandy Beach had 57,385 visitors one year, 49,275 the next, and 53,658 the next. How many visitors did Sandy Beach have in all three years?	Jose loves to read books. He read books that were 449 pages, 764 pages, 502 pages, and 393 pages this summer. How many pages is that in all?

Name(s): _____

Oh, What's the Difference?

You'll see the difference when you solve three
subtraction problems and get Tic-Tac-Math!

825 − 58	1,600 − 443	67,312 − 38,350
Sabrina won the big prize in a raffle—$450! She spent $338 of it on a GameStation 3 system and video games. How much money did Sabrina have left after that?	Isabella had a bake sale. In one hour, Isabella has sold 109 of her 567 ultra-fudge-chip cupcakes. How many cupcakes does Isabella have left?	The Ortiz family were driving from their house to their friends' house 398 miles away. After 119 miles, they took a break for lunch. How many more miles did they have to drive to get to their friends?
In the summer, all of Dennis's freckles came out. He had a total of 702 freckles. In the winter, his mom counted 589 freckles. How many more freckles did Dennis have in the summer than in the winter?	Caroline wanted to make the world's largest chocolate-chip cookie with 72,390 chips in it. But she ran out of chips after she had used 55,431. How many more chocolate chips does she need to buy?	Tabitha had 90,002 N&N chocolate candies. Her brother snuck into her room and ate 1,735 of them! How many candies were left?

Name(s): _____

Master Multiplication!

Flex your mental muscles and solve three multiplication problems to get Tic-Tac-Math!

85 x 18	93 x 17	45 x 13
There are 324 pear trees in an orchard. Each tree has exactly 89 pears on it. How many pears are there on all of the trees together?	The Fuzzy Wuzzies' new CD has sold 562 copies. Each CD cost $18. What's the total amount collected for all of those CDs?	Oh, no! The whole fifth-grade class broke out in cheetah pox. There are 57 students and each student has exactly 264 cheetah pox spots on his or her body. How many spots does the fifth-grade class have altogether?
On a clear night, the sky was filled with stars. Ahmad counted 499 of them. If Ahmad made 23 wishes on each star that he saw, how many wishes did he make altogether?	Ming loves to ride her bicycle. Every day she rides 12 miles. How many miles does she ride in a 365-day year?	There were 257 teens at The Stinky Cheese concert. If each teen screamed 83 times during the concert, how many screams were there in all?

Name(s): _____

Dive Into Division!

Make a splash! Solve three division problems to get Tic-Tac-Math!

$450 \div 15 =$	$6{,}644 \div 22 =$	$7{,}245 \div 35 =$
$38 \overline{)8{,}952}$	$46 \overline{)67{,}904}$	Juan is training to run in a marathon. He is supposed to run 150 miles in 6 weeks. If he runs the same number of miles each week, how many miles will he run each week?
Luigi's Pizzeria puts 18 slices of pepperoni on each pepperoni pizza that is ordered. They used up all 1,746 slices of pepperoni they had one week. How many pepperoni pizzas did they make that week?	Carla had 595 heart candies that she wanted to divide up evenly into 20 goody bags for Valentine's Day. How many heart candies will each goody bag have? How many candies will Carla have left over?	Milo's fifth-grade class had a total of 109 students. They were all going to a play. Each row holds 15 people. How many full rows would Milo's class take up? How many students would partially fill another row?

Name(s): _____

Divisibility Rules Rule!

The Queen of Divisibility Rules challenges you to solve three problems to get Tic-Tac-Math!

Which of the following numbers are factors of 885? 2 3 4 5 9	Which of the following numbers are factors of 9,999? 2 3 4 5 9	Which of the following numbers are factors of 7,070? 2 3 4 5 9 10
What number must go in the blank to make a four-digit number that is divisible by 6? 671____	What number between 10 and 20 is divisible by both 3 and 5?	What number(s) must go in the blank to make the number divisible by 3? 7____2
What is the smallest 3-digit number that is divisible by 2, 3, 4, and 6?	What number between 40 and 50 is divisible by both 2 and 11?	Name the prime number between 20 and 30 whose ones digit is 7 greater than its tens digit.

Scholastic • Tic-Tac-Math: Grades 5 & Up

Name(s): _____

The Factor Factory

Get to work! Solve three problems to get Tic-Tac-Math!

List all of the factors of 8 from least to greatest.	List all of the factors of 14 from least to greatest.	List all of the factors of 30 from least to greatest.
Which of the following numbers are prime? 7 9 15 21 29 33	Which of the following numbers are prime? 39 53 47 35 37 41	List all of the prime numbers between 70 and 99.
What is the greatest common factor of 8 and 12?	What is the greatest common factor of 27 and 9?	What is the greatest common factor of 45 and 60?

Name(s): _____

Mad About Multiples!

Do you find multiples mesmerizing? Solve three problems to get Tic-Tac-Math!

Which of the following are multiples of 5?

20   52   35

23   30

Which of the following are multiples of 6?

18   30   16

25   24

Which of the following are multiples of 3?

29   31   52

78   102

What is the least common multiple of 7 and 4?

What is the least common multiple of 24 and 12?

What is the least common multiple of 15 and 21?

Two dogs are sitting next to each other. Starting now, one dog will bark every 3 seconds and the other dog will bark every 5 seconds. When is the next time both dogs will bark at the same time?

Barney and Julia are both very tired. Starting now, Barney will yawn every 8 seconds and Julia will yawn every 4 seconds. When is the next time both of them will yawn at the same time?

Glenda and Penny are doing a sack race. Glenda jumps forward 18 inches each time she jumps. Each of Penny's hops is 15 inches. How far from the starting line will it be when Glenda and Penny have both landed at the same distance?

Name(s): _____

Deci-mental Powers

Do you have deci-mental powers? Prove it by solving three problems to get Tic-Tac-Math!

Write forty-eight hundredths as a decimal number.	Write 2.73 in words.	Write fifty-eight and three hundred seventy-nine thousandths as a decimal number.
Think of a number with 8 in its thousandths place, 5 in its ones place, 0 in its hundredths place, and 4 in its tenths place. What number is it?	Write $10 + 0.1 + 0.07 + 0.002$ in standard form.	Write 26.731 in expanded form.
Think of a number that ends at the hundredths place, is 0.2 when rounded to the tenths place, and has digits that add up to 7. What number is it?	Think of a number that ends at the thousandths place, is 0.68 when rounded to the hundredths place, and has digits that add up to 17. What number is it?	Think of two numbers. When you add them, you get 6.5. When you multiply them, you get 0.64. What are the two numbers?

Name(s): _____

Order in the Court!

Now that we've got your attention, solve three problems to get Tic-Tac-Math!

Fill in the box with <, >, or =.

0.394 ▢ 0.439

Fill in the box with <, >, or =.

0.738 ▢ 0.74

Fill in the box with <, >, or =.

3.61 ▢ 3.608

Order these values from greatest to least:

7.281   7.29   7.284

Order these values from least to greatest:

0.5092   0.509

0.513   0.5089

Which statement below is true?

a) 200.2 > 200.222

b) 0.33 < 3.3

c) 15 = 1.50

d) 30.0 > 50

Mr. Buff, the gym teacher, recorded the following times for a group of students running across the school's field: 10.5 seconds, 10.89 seconds, 9.00 seconds, 10.29 seconds, and 11.2 seconds. Put the students' times in order from fastest to slowest.

Tamiqua is thinking of a number between 2.785 and 2.8. Which of these numbers could she be thinking of?

a) 2.79   c) 2.85

b) 2.75   d) 2.779

Name the decimal that is halfway between 0.005 and 0.006.

Name(s): _____

"Sum" More Decimals

Adding decimals is no clowning matter! Solve three problems to get Tic-Tac-Math!

4.3 + 2.5 =	6.8 + 3.65 =	49.38 + 16.01 =
In the frog-jumping contest, Hannah's frog jumped 48.7 cm on his first try and 35.9 cm on his second try. How far did Hannah's frog jump in all?	Jordan was 177.8-cm tall when school started in September. But by June, he had grown 20.5 cm more. How tall was Jordan in June?	Francisco jumped 180.5 cm on his first standing long jump. On his second jump, he jumped 200.2 cm. How far did he jump in all?
Beatrice made a gigantic batch of peanut-butter chip cookies. She mixed in 207.75 pounds of flour, 89.75 pounds of butter, and 92.5 pounds of brown sugar. How many pounds of ingredients is that?	For this year's Halloween costume, Forrest got a clown outfit for $41.89, big floppy shoes for $23.50, and a multi-colored wig for $35.99. How much did he spend in all?	A policewoman monitored the speed of passing cars. A green minivan cruised by at 50.8 mph. Next, a silver sports car zoomed by at 44.7 mph faster than the minivan. How fast was the sports car traveling?

Name(s): _____

Decimal Deli

People order strange amounts of food at this deli.
Solve three problems to get Tic-Tac-Math!

7.65 – 4.3 =

8.25 – 1.4 =

67.39 – 4.934 =

Paula orders 3.75 pounds of macaroni salad and 2.25 pounds of coleslaw. How many more pounds of macaroni salad does she have than coleslaw?

Robby orders 1.33 pounds of salami, then asks the clerk to put 0.425 pounds of it back. How much salami did Robby end up with?

Anne-Marie orders 0.75 pounds of American cheese and 2.478 pounds of bologna. How many more pounds of bologna does she have than cheese?

Gabriella orders 27.152 pounds of olive loaf. Right after that, Christopher orders 35.08 pounds of it! How much more olive loaf did Christopher order?

If you buy over 2 pounds of roast beef, you get a free pound of mystery meat! You've already ordered 1.9823 pounds. How much more roast beef would you need to buy to get the mystery meat?

The clerk puts 2.789 pounds of turkey on the scale, then another 1.86 pounds. Then he takes 0.3487 pounds off. How many pounds of turkey are left on the scale?

Name(s): _____

It's Time(s) for Decimals!

Solve three decimal multiplication problems to get Tic-Tac-Math!

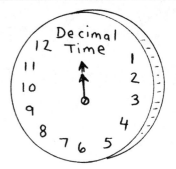

$8.9 \times 5 =$

$0.35 \times 0.7 =$

$4.8 \times 0.62 =$

Fred Funstone ordered 9 Bronto burgers. Each one costs $6.98. What's the total price of the burgers?

The length of each side of a regular decagon (10-sided polygon) is 7.98 inches. What is the perimeter of the decagon?

Speedy Sabrina runs a mile in 6.4 minutes. If she continues at this pace, how long will it take her to run 9.7 miles?

Sweet Susie took 15 of her friends to the movies. Each ticket cost $9.50, and everyone had a large popcorn for $2.95. What was the total cost for the movie tickets and popcorn? (Remember: There are 16 girls altogether!)

When Carlos saw that Sweet Treats had his favorite—chocolate fudge with multi-colored chocolate chips—he bought 9.5 pounds of it at $8.99 a pound. How much did he spend on fudge? Round your answer to the nearest cent.

Sandy bought 3.5 pounds of potato salad at $3.75 a pound and 4.04 pounds of macaroni salad at $4.15 a pound. How much did Sandy pay for both salads? Round your answer to the nearest cent.

Name(s): _____

Dare to Divide Decimals!

Don't try this stunt at home! Instead, solve three decimal division problems to get Tic-Tac-Math!

$4\overline{)7.6}$

$5\overline{)9.8}$

$4.5\overline{)103.5}$

$6\overline{)12.9}$

$0.16\overline{)4.38}$

Ingrid bought a 6-pack of genuine artificially flavored kumquat soda for $1.68. How much is each can of soda?

Kenny runs the same distance every day. If he runs a total of 24 miles every 5 days, how many miles does he run each day?

Gabriel has a large jar full of quarters. He finally decided to put them in rolls and take them to the bank. He had $10.50 worth of quarters. How many quarters did he have?

Fanny gave out 26.4 pounds of delicious fudge to her family and friends. She gave each person a 0.4-pound bag of fudge. How many bags of fudge did Fanny give out in all?

Name(s): _____

Make Sense of Cents!

How savvy are you with money?
Solve three cash-counting problems
to get Tic-Tac-Math!

You dump out your piggy bank to find 5 quarters, 3 dimes, 2 nickels, and 3 pennies. How much money do you have?

Max has 31 dimes and 18 nickels. How much money does he have?

Tanya has 15 coins worth $.72. The coins are all dimes, nickels, and pennies. What are the coins?

Norma Jean has a total of 24 coins, consisting of just quarters and nickels. The coins total $3.40. How many of them are quarters?

Pablo has 90 cents in coins consisting of only quarters, dimes, and nickels. What is the least number of coins he could have? Name them.

List all the possible ways to make 28 cents. Make a chart with labels for quarters, dimes, nickels, and pennies to help you keep track of all the ways.

The 182 sixth graders at Hammer Middle School are going to the museum. The entrance fee is $1.75 per student and $3.25 per adult. The bus fee is $189 per bus. Each bus holds 44 people. What is the total cost for the students and 14 adults to visit the museum?

A pair of pants and a shirt cost $75 altogether. If the shirt costs $15 more than the pants, how much do the pants cost?

Jennifer is treating her parents and younger sister to the school play. Tickets cost $6.00 for adults and $2.25 for kids. Jennifer earns $2.75 an hour baby-sitting. How many hours will she have to work to earn enough money for the tickets? (Remember, Jennifer needs a kid's ticket too!)

Name(s): _____

Fractions Beyond Compare

Fractions are simply gorgeous! Solve three problems to get Tic-Tac-Math!

Which fractions are greater than $\frac{1}{2}$? $\quad\frac{5}{12}\quad\frac{10}{18}\quad\frac{6}{14}\quad\frac{3}{4}$ $\quad\frac{15}{28}\quad\frac{9}{16}\quad\frac{4}{10}\quad\frac{21}{50}$	Which fractions are less than $\frac{1}{2}$? $\quad\frac{1}{7}\quad\frac{3}{6}\quad\frac{15}{29}$ $\quad\frac{56}{60}\quad\frac{6}{18}$	Write three fractions that are equivalent to $\frac{1}{2}$ using the denominators 20, 44, and 72.
Hortence is really hungry. Which amount of pizza should she eat if she wants to eat more — $\frac{2}{4}$ of a pizza or $\frac{2}{3}$ of a pizza?	Marco studied for $\frac{14}{16}$ of an hour and Melissa studied for $\frac{3}{4}$ of an hour. Who studied longer?	Frangelica swam $2\frac{1}{2}$ laps at the pool, while her sister Bailey swam $2\frac{2}{4}$ laps. Who swam more?
Bekah ran $\frac{4}{5}$ of a mile and Jeff ran $\frac{2}{3}$ of a mile. Who ran more?	Paula Sue completed $\frac{7}{8}$ of her homework, and Janet Lynn completed $\frac{15}{20}$ of her homework. Who did a greater portion of her homework?	Roberto skied $4\frac{3}{5}$ miles on the cross-country trails, while his brother Pascal skied $4\frac{9}{10}$ miles. Who skied a greater distance?

Scholastic • Tic-Tac-Math: Grades 5 & Up

Name(s): _____

Add "Sum" Fractions!

You just "half" to solve three fraction addition problems to get Tic-Tac-Math! Write all answers in simplest form.

$\frac{1}{6} + \frac{4}{6} =$	$2\frac{3}{8} + 1\frac{2}{8} =$	$\frac{4}{9} + \frac{1}{3} =$
$\frac{5}{6} + \frac{3}{4} =$	$8\frac{7}{8} + 2\frac{2}{5} =$	$5\frac{1}{6} + 8\frac{3}{8} + 2\frac{1}{3} =$
Daniel made a pan of butterscotch brownies. He ate $\frac{1}{4}$ of the pan on Tuesday and $\frac{3}{8}$ of the pan on Friday. How much of the pan did Daniel eat on those two days together?	Nina was $48\frac{3}{4}$ inches tall on her birthday last year. This year she grew $1\frac{5}{8}$ inches more. How tall is she now?	On Monday morning, Heather ran $5\frac{1}{3}$ miles. On Wednesday morning she ran $6\frac{3}{4}$ miles, and on Friday morning she ran $5\frac{7}{8}$ miles. How many miles did she run altogether?

Name(s): _____

Fraction Leftovers

What's left over when you subtract these mixed numbers? Solve three problems to get Tic-Tac-Math!

$\frac{3}{4} - \frac{1}{4} =$	$7\frac{3}{5} - 3\frac{1}{5} =$	$\frac{7}{8} - \frac{3}{16} =$
$8\frac{7}{10} - 3\frac{2}{5} =$	$9\frac{3}{4} - 3\frac{1}{2} =$	Sasha was shocked to realize that she had collected $10\frac{7}{8}$ pounds of Halloween candy. So she brought $5\frac{5}{8}$ pounds of it to school to share with her friends. How much candy did Sasha have left?
Paulina's butterscotch and chocolate-chip brownies were so good that she made 5 large pans of them for her holiday party. After the party, she only had $1\frac{3}{5}$ pans of brownies left. What fraction of the brownies did her guests eat?	Derek intended to cut a piece of wood $12\frac{5}{8}$ " long. By mistake, he cut a piece $11\frac{1}{4}$ " long. How much shorter was the piece than it was supposed to be?	Max was planning to run $10\frac{1}{4}$ miles on Saturday. He ran $3\frac{4}{5}$ miles before twisting his ankle. How many miles was Max short of his goal?

Name(s): _____

Recipe for Multipli-Fractions

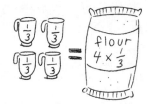

Get cooking on solving three fraction multiplication problems to get Tic-Tac-Math!

$\frac{3}{8} \times 3 =$	$\frac{4}{5} \times \frac{1}{3} =$	$\frac{6}{11} \times \frac{5}{6} =$
$7\frac{2}{5} \times 3 =$	$3\frac{1}{2} \times 6 =$	$2\frac{1}{2} \times 3\frac{3}{8} =$
A recipe calls for $\frac{3}{4}$ cup of flour. If Jacob triples the recipe, how much flour will he use?	Patrick usually jogs $1\frac{1}{2}$ miles each morning. But yesterday, he jogged only $\frac{1}{3}$ as far. How far did Patrick jog yesterday?	Tammy's tiny doll is $2\frac{2}{3}$ " tall. Her big doll is $3\frac{6}{7}$ times as tall. How tall is her big doll?

Name(s): _____

I Will Divide This Fraction in Half!

You don't have to be a magician to divide fractions. Simply solve three problems to get Tic-Tac-Math! Express answers in simplest form.

$15 \div \frac{1}{2} =$	$2 \div \frac{1}{8} =$	$\frac{3}{9} \div \frac{2}{5} =$
$2\frac{1}{2} \div \frac{1}{8} =$	$5 \div \frac{2}{3} =$	$32\frac{5}{8} \div 3\frac{5}{8} =$
Hortence has 12 yards of ribbon, which she plans to cut into even strips of $\frac{3}{4}$-yard long. How many strips will she have?	Anna had $6\frac{3}{4}$ pounds of jelly beans, which she divided evenly into 108 bags. How many pounds of jelly beans were in each bag?	Gina made $8\frac{1}{2}$ pounds of fudge, which she was putting into $\frac{3}{4}$-pound bags to sell at the school bake sale. How many bags of fudge can she fill? How much fudge will she have left over?

Name(s): _____

Ratio Rodeo

Yee-haw! See if you can rustle up some ratios by solving three problems to get Tic-Tac-Math! Express your answers in simplest form.

A box of chocolates has 8 solid chocolates and 4 chocolate-covered caramels. What is the ratio of chocolate-covered caramels to solid chocolates?

In a jar, there are 6 red jelly beans, 3 yellow jelly beans, and 9 orange jelly beans. What is the ratio of red jelly beans to orange jelly beans?

In a jar, there are 5 red M&Ants, 8 yellow ones, and 4 orange ones. What is the ratio of orange M&Ants to yellow ones?

Solve the following proportion:

$$\frac{12}{24} = \frac{60}{y}$$

Solve the following proportion:

$$\frac{18}{x} = \frac{30}{100}$$

Solve the following proportion:

$$\frac{x}{50} = \frac{18}{30}$$

The ratio of oil to vinegar in salad dressing is 3 to 1. If you make a large batch of salad dressing with $\frac{3}{4}$ cup of vinegar, how much oil do you need?

A map's scale is $\frac{1}{4}$ inch = 6 miles. The remote island of Boogie Woogie is 12 miles by 21 miles. What would be the island's dimensions on the map? Write proportions to solve.

12% of 800 toy cars are defective. Solve the following proportion to find out how many cars are defective.

$$\frac{12}{100} = \frac{x}{800}$$

Name(s): _____

Percent Scents?

Skunks stink at finding the percent of a number.
Follow your nose and solve three percent problems
to get Tic-Tac-Math!

What is 10% of 80?	What is 20% of 660?	Stanley only got 80% of the 80 questions on the geography test correct. How many problems did he get right? How many did he get wrong?
What is 18% of 900?	What is 28% of 175?	Conceited Carlos claimed that he would dance with 75% of the 260 girls at the dance. If Carlos fulfilled his claim, how many girls did he dance with?
What is 38% of 230?	Vera bought a black velvet dress because it was on sale for 25% off. The original price was $73. How much did Vera save?	Roger was the 1,000th customer at The Dill Pickle, so he received a coupon for 15% off his purchase. Roger spent $167.99 on groceries. How much money did he save with the coupon? Round your answer to the nearest cent.

Name(s): _____

Percent Power!

Join the battle for truth, justice, and correct calculations!
Solve three percent problems to get Tic-Tac-Math!
If necessary, round your answers to the nearest
whole percent.

48 is what percent of 200?	21 is what percent of 25?	Elizabeth collected baseball caps. She had 360 of them altogether. 18 of them had no writing on them. What percent of her caps had no writing on them?
9 is what percent of 36?	63 is what percent of 72?	Joe took 32 pictures at the school's talent show. Exactly 10 of them came out too dark. What percent of them were too dark?
12 is what percent of 52?	Oriana made 15 of the 35 hoop shots she took. What percent of the shots did she make?	Antoine read 105 of the 673 pages of *Invasion of the Smelly Jelly Rolls* before his mom told him to turn off the lights and go to sleep. What percent of the book did he read?

Name(s): _____

Donut Wholes

See how we arranged these donuts to look like a percent sign? We'll give you a number and a percent, you tell us what other number that's a percent of. Solve three problems to get Tic-Tac-Math!

7 is 10% of what number?	80 is 25% of what number?	Annie earned A's on 8 of her math tests last year. These 8 tests represent 50% of the total number of math tests she took. How many math tests did she take?
Poor Betty Croaker burned a full one dozen of the cookies she baked. If these burnt cookies represent 20% of all of the cookies Betty baked, how many cookies did Betty bake?	220 is 40% of what number?	Matthew got 15 books for his birthday. These books represent 60% of all of his presents. How many presents did Matthew receive?
Talya ate 76% of the jelly beans in the bag. If she ate 57 jelly beans, how many jelly beans were in the bag to begin with?	Three of the cast members of the fifth-grade play were home sick with the flamingo flu. If these children represent 6% of the students in the fifth-grade play, how many students are in the fifth-grade play?	Harry spent 15% of his paycheck on clothes. If he spent $324 on clothes, how much was his paycheck?

Name(s): _____

We're All Equal!

Fractions, decimals, and percents all express parts
of a whole. Solve three problems to get Tic-Tac-Math!

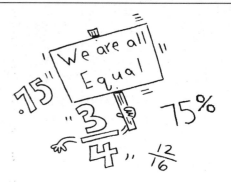

What is the decimal equivalent of $\frac{1}{4}$?	What is the fraction equivalent of 0.6 (in simplest form)?	What is the percent equivalent of $\frac{7}{10}$?
Which is greatest? 40% $\frac{5}{8}$ 0.6	Which is least? $\frac{1}{5}$ 15% 0.1	Which is greatest? 35% $\frac{8}{25}$ $\frac{2}{5}$ 0.39
Order the set from least to greatest: $\frac{7}{20}$ 0.38 24% 9.8% $\frac{3}{8}$ 0.52	Order the set from greatest to least: 0.74 47.5% 0.48 $\frac{1}{2}$ $\frac{3}{10}$ 0.6	Order the set from least to greatest: 0.55 $\frac{1}{10}$ 45% $\frac{1}{3}$ $\frac{1}{5}$ 0.35 0.05 25%

Name(s): _____

Super Powers

Don't be fooled by an exponent's small size—it's really packed with power! You'll see what we mean when you solve three problems to get Tic-Tac-Math!

Express 8^2 in standard form.	Express 3^3 in standard form.	Express 4^5 in standard form.
Express 10^{-4} in standard form.	Express 2.5×10^{-2} in standard form.	Express 0.007 using scientific notation.
Express 0.0308 using scientific notation.	Express the standard form of $7 \times 10^3 + 5 \times 10^2 + 3 \times 10^1$.	Express the standard form of $5 \times 10^2 + 2 \times 10^{-1} + 8 \times 10^{-4}$.

Name(s): _____

Absolutely Positive!

Being negative isn't so bad. Negative numbers are actually pretty cool. Solve three integer problems to get Tic-Tac-Math!

What is the absolute value of –8?	What is the absolute value of –13?	Fill in the box with <, >, or =. –3 ☐ 2
Fill in the box with <, >, or =. 6 ☐ –5	Imagine a number line with negative numbers to the left of zero and positive numbers to its right. If you start on +7 and move three spaces to the right, on what number will you land?	What is the sum of –3 and +7?
Find the sum: –4 + –3 + –11	Talia added –4 + –5 + 8 and got –17. She made an error. What error do you think she made? What is the correct answer?	What number should you add to –8 to get +12?

Name(s): _____

Meet Patty Pattern!

Patty Pattern loves creating patterns. Solve three pattern problems to get Tic-Tac-Math!

Find the next three numbers in the pattern below. Then explain the pattern in words.

15, 20, 25, 30

____, ____, ____

Find the next three numbers in the pattern below. Then explain the pattern in words.

8, 17, 26, 35

____, ____, ____

Find the next three numbers in the pattern below. Then explain the pattern in words.

74, 71, 68, 65

____, ____, ____

Find the next three numbers in the pattern below. Then explain the pattern in words.

19, 14, 15, 10, 11

____, ____, ____

Find the next three numbers in the pattern below. Then explain the pattern in words.

17, 14, 12, 9, 7

____, ____, ____

Find the next three numbers in the pattern below. Then explain the pattern in words.

3, 6, 12, 24

____, ____, ____

Find the next three numbers in the pattern below. Then explain the pattern in words.

512, 256, 128

____, ____, ____

Find the next three numbers in the pattern below. Then explain the pattern in words.

–15, –12, –9, –6

____, ____, ____

Find the next three numbers in the pattern below. Then explain the pattern in words.

–40, –30, –32, –33,

–23, –25, –26, –16

____, ____, ____

Scholastic • Tic-Tac-Math: Grades 5 & Up

Name(s): _____

Three Cheers for Decimal Patterns!

Hip-hip-hooray! These girls are rooting for you to solve three pattern problems and get Tic-Tac-Math!

Find the next three numbers in the pattern below. Then explain the pattern in words.

5.1, 5.2, 5.3

____, ____, ____

Find the next three numbers in the pattern below. Then explain the pattern in words.

10.75, 10.65, 10.55

____, ____, ____

Find the next three numbers in the pattern below. Then explain the pattern in words.

9.1, 8.8, 8.5, 8.2

____, ____, ____

Find the next three numbers in the pattern below. Then explain the pattern in words.

0.2, 7.9, 15.6, 23.3

____, ____, ____

Find the next three numbers in the pattern below. Then explain the pattern in words.

0.2, 0.22, 0.24, 0.26

____, ____, ____

Find the next three numbers in the pattern below. Then explain the pattern in words.

0.07, 0.08, 0.09

____, ____, ____

Find the next three numbers in the pattern below. Then explain the pattern in words.

0.5, 0.05, 0.005

____, ____, ____

Find the next three numbers in the pattern below. Then explain the pattern in words.

0.2, 0.6, 1.8

____, ____, ____

Find the next three numbers in the pattern below. Then explain the pattern in words.

8.25, 7.65, 7.05

____, ____, ____

Name(s): _____

I Detect a Pattern

Look for clues to help you uncover the next numbers in each pattern. Solve three pattern problems to get Tic-Tac-Math!

Find the next three numbers in the pattern below. Then explain the pattern in words.

$$\frac{1}{8}, \ \frac{3}{8}, \ \frac{5}{8}, \ \frac{7}{8}$$

____, ____, ____

Find the next three numbers in the pattern below. Then explain the pattern in words.

$$\frac{4}{3}, \ \frac{7}{3}, \ \frac{10}{3}$$

____, ____, ____

Find the next three numbers in the pattern below. Then explain the pattern in words.

$$\frac{1}{2}, \ \frac{1}{4}, \ \frac{1}{8}, \ \frac{1}{16}, \ \frac{1}{32}$$

____, ____, ____

Find the next three numbers in the pattern below. Then explain the pattern in words.

$$\frac{3}{7}, \ \frac{3}{14}, \ \frac{3}{28}, \ \frac{3}{56}$$

____, ____, ____

Find the next three numbers in the pattern below. Then explain the pattern in words.

$$2\frac{1}{4}, \ 2, \ 1\frac{3}{4}$$

____, ____, ____

Find the next three numbers in the pattern below. Then explain the pattern in words.

$$\frac{1}{5}, \ \frac{4}{5}, \ \frac{2}{5}, \ 1, \ \frac{3}{5}, \ 1\frac{1}{5}$$

____, ____, ____

Find the next three numbers in the pattern below. Then explain the pattern in words.

$$2\frac{3}{5}, \ 2\frac{1}{5}, \ 2\frac{2}{5}, \ 2, \ 2\frac{1}{5}$$

____, ____, ____

Find the next three numbers in the pattern below. Then explain the pattern in words.

$$3\frac{3}{8}, \ 3\frac{5}{8}, \ 3\frac{1}{2}, \ 3\frac{3}{4},$$

$$3\frac{5}{8}, \ 3\frac{7}{8}, \ 3\frac{3}{4}, \ 4$$

____, ____, ____

Find the next three numbers in the pattern below. Then explain the pattern in words.

$$\frac{1}{3}, \ \frac{2}{3}, \ 1\frac{1}{3}, \ 2\frac{2}{3}, \ 5\frac{1}{3}$$

____, ____, ____

Name(s): _____

Pass the Pattern Table!

Fill in the blanks in each function table to show the relationship between the numbers in column A and column B. Solve three to get Tic-Tac-Math!

A	B
4	7
0	3
16	19
11	
5	
	12

A	B
18	13
5	0
10	
14	
	8

A	B
2	20
5	50
7	
3	
	300

A	B
5	7
8	10
15	
	12
0.5	

A	B
2	6
5	15
0	0
3	
	-30

A	B
$\frac{1}{8}$	$\frac{3}{8}$
$\frac{3}{4}$	1
$\frac{1}{2}$	$\frac{3}{4}$
2	
	$\frac{7}{8}$
$\frac{9}{8}$	

A	B
4	11
0	-1
3	8
10	
	5

A	B
7	15
2	5
0	1
10	
	-3

A	B
4	5
1	-1
0	-3
-2	
	2

Name(s): _____

x Marks the Spot!

You've found it—the secret to evaluating variable expressions. Solve three problems to get Tic-Tac-Math!

$x + 7$, where $x = 8$	$3x$, where $x = 4$	$x \div 5$, where $x = 30$
$2x - 3$, where $x = 7$	$1 + 4x$, where $x = 2$	$13x - 28$, where $x = 5$
$9x + 6 - 5x$, where $x = -1$	A hot dog costs $1.27 more than twice the price of a soda. Write an expression that shows the price of a hot dog in relation to the price of a soda. Then evaluate where a soda costs $.99.	A super sundae costs $.88 less than 3 times the price of a single cone. Write an expression that shows the price of a super sundae in relation to the price of a single cone. Then evaluate where a single cone costs $1.39.

Scholastic • Tic-Tac-Math: Grades 5 & Up

Name(s): _____

Simplifying Sampler

Evaluate each fraction for x to solve three problems and get Tic-Tac-Math! Write each fraction in simplest form.

$\dfrac{x}{x + 10}$ where $x = 5$	$\dfrac{x}{20}$ where $x = 10$	$\dfrac{x}{x}$ where $x = 145$
$\dfrac{x - 5}{x + 5}$ where $x = 10$	$\dfrac{3}{x + 7}$ where $x = 5$	$\dfrac{2 + x}{18 - x}$ where $x = 2$
$\dfrac{4x}{3x + 7}$ where $x = 5$	$\dfrac{3x - 5}{8x + 2}$ where $x = 7$	$\dfrac{2x - 5}{7x + 2}$ where $x = 4$

Name(s): _____

FraXions

Solve for x in three fraction variable problems to get Tic-Tac-Math!
(Hint: Use proportions to solve these.)

Find the value of x that will make this equation true: $$\frac{x}{x+4} = \frac{1}{2}$$	Find the value of x that will make this equation true: $$\frac{x}{10} = \frac{1}{5}$$	Find the value of x that will make this equation true: $$\frac{x+1}{10} = \frac{1}{2}$$
Find the value of x that will make this equation true: $$\frac{3}{x+7} = \frac{1}{3}$$	Find the value of x that will make this equation true: $$\frac{x}{2x+4} = \frac{2}{5}$$	A fraction's denominator is 8 less than twice its numerator. If the fraction is equivalent to $\frac{3}{5}$, what is the fraction?
The denominator of a fraction is 3 more than its numerator. The fraction is equivalent to $\frac{3}{4}$. What is the fraction?	The denominator of a fraction is 1 less than 9 times the numerator. If the fraction is equivalent to $\frac{5}{40}$, what is the numerator of the fraction?	If a fraction's denominator is 1 more than 3 times its numerator, and the fraction is equivalent to $\frac{12}{39}$, what is the fraction?

Name(s): _____

Give *y* a Try!

Write an algebraic equation to represent and solve each problem. Solve three problems to get Tic-Tac-Math!

A rectangle's length is *y* cm. Its width is 5 cm. Its perimeter is 34 cm. Find the length of the rectangle.

A rectangle's length is *y* cm. Its width is 2 cm. The perimeter is 10 cm. Find the rectangle's width.

Harold's dad is 3 times his age. The sum of Harold's age and his father's age is 60 years. How old is Harold? How old is his dad?

Oriana is 5 years older than her brother Francisco. The sum of their ages is 27. How old is each child?

Ella is twice Bella's age, and Stella is three times Bella's age. The difference between Stella's and Bella's ages is 8 years. How old is each girl?

Harlan's dad is 3 years more than 4 times Harlan's age. The difference in their ages is 30 years. How old is Harlan? How old is his dad?

Sally has twice as many hair ribbons as Natasha. Bethany has 3 less than Sally. The sum of all three girls' ribbons is 32. How many hair ribbons does each girl have?

Janet bought 3 dozen donuts from Delectable Donuts. She bought 3 times as many honey-dipped as plain. She bought 6 fewer chocolate-frosted than honey-dipped. How many of each did she buy?

Ty, Malcolm, and Fred were playing basketball. Malcolm made 2 more baskets than Ty, and Fred made 4 more than twice the number that Ty made. Together, the boys made 42 baskets. How many baskets did each boy make?

Name(s): _____

Try Using a Table!

These problems may look tough. Make a table or chart and use a guess-and-check strategy to find the solution. Solve three problems to get Tic-Tac-Math!

You have 81 cents in coins. If you have 7 coins, what coins do you have?

Gary sells $10 raffle tickets for a jet ski. He also sells $4 raffle tickets for a $100 gift certificate at Wally's Winter Wonderland. If Gary sells 25 tickets and collects $160, how many of each raffle ticket does he sell?

There were 39 creatures in Sam's drawing. He drew 2-legged Gooberlings and 4-legged Farfalles. If there were a total of 122 legs in the drawing, how many Gooberlings and Farfalles were in Sam's picture?

Grace drew a total of 20 5-petaled flowers and 7-petaled flowers. Her drawing contained 124 petals. How many 5-petaled flowers and how many 7-petaled flowers did Grace draw?

Alex has $3.65 in nickels and dimes. He has 45 coins. How many of each coin does he have?

Jada has a total of 21 coins, only dimes and quarters. She has $3.15. How many of each coin does she have?

Laura had exactly $1 in change. She had only quarters, dimes, and nickels. If she had 12 coins, how many of each coin did she have?

Ames had $1.15 in change in pennies, nickels, and dimes. He had 18 coins. How many of each did he have?

June made a pattern with 8 pattern blocks. She used triangles, squares, and hexagons. There were 32 sides in all. How many of each shape were there?

Name(s): _____

Mean and Median à la Mode

Yum! Look at the tasty mean, median, and mode problems.
Solve three to get Tic-Tac-Math!

Find the median of the following data: 7, 12, 15, 12, 5, 6, 4, 1	Find the median, mode, and range of the following lengths of pieces of wood (all the measurements are in inches): 4, 3, 8, 3, 5, 2, 3	Find the mean, median, mode, and range of the following numbers: 6, 1, 3, 1, 5
What whole number must the missing piece of data be to have a range of 15? 14, ____, 9, 12, 2, 2, 8, 2, 1	What must the missing piece of data be to have a mode of 3? 5, 2, 3, 3, 2, 4, ____	What must the missing piece of data be to have a mean of 8? 7, 12, ____, 3, 11
What must the missing piece of data be to have a mean of 30? 20, 30, 50, 40, ____	What must the missing piece of data be to have a mean of 20? 18, 11, 7, 15, 32, 27, ____	What must the missing piece of data be to have a mean of 33? 51, 52, ____, 23, 21, 17, 37, 45

Scholastic • *Tic-Tac-Math: Grades 5 & Up*

Name(s): _____

Above-Average Kids

Give these average problems your best shot.
Solve three problems to get Tic-Tac-Math!

In last week's baseball game, Henry scored 7 runs, Parker scored 4, Dominick 3, and Bill 2. What was their mean score? What was their median score?

Hillary, Bethany, and Hannah earn money by raking leaves. One weekend, Hillary earned $95, Bethany earned $57, and Hannah earned $100. What was the mean number of dollars the three girls earned?

Franny sorted a big bag of jelly beans by color. She found 37 red, 49 yellow, 18 white, 53 black, 39 orange, and 56 green. What was the mean number of each color? What was the median number?

Your math teacher will let you choose whether you will receive the mean or the median of your test scores on your report card. These are your test scores: 88, 90, 80, 63, 73, 72, and 87. Should you choose the mean or the median?

Lily and her friends have a party so they could trade barrettes, hair ties, and headbands. Carla brought 87 hair accessories, Brenda brought 43, Olga's overstuffed bag held 91, and Lily had 49. What was the range of hair accessories at the party?

Last summer the Sampson triplets each read 7 books. Their older brother read 23 mystery books. What was the mean number of books the Sampson children read? What was the median number of books?

At the game, shouts came from all over the stadium—20 from one area, 12 from another, 17 from the top rows, 17 from the left section, 29 from the bottom rows, 25 from the right section, and 18 from the center. What was the median number of shouts? What was the range? What was the mode?

For the bake sale, Kyle brought 3 dozen peanut-butter brownies, Hannah brought $2\frac{1}{2}$ dozen chocolate-chip ones, Mona brought $2\frac{1}{2}$ dozen plain brownies, and Carl made 56 rainbow-sprinkled brownies. What was the mean number of brownies? What was the median number?

Tyler wanted to know how many CDs each of his friends owns. Here's the number of CDs each of his friends has: 8, 11, 5, 2, 5, 7, 1, 15, and 18. What is the mean and median number of CDs that Tyler's friends own? What is the mode? What is the range?

Scholastic • Tic-Tac-Math: Grades 5 & Up

Name(s): _____

What's Your Probability Ability?

Chances are, you can solve three problems to get Tic-Tac-Math!

You roll one die. What is the probability that you roll an odd number?	You roll one die. What is the probability that you roll a number greater than 4?	In a bag there are 7 green marbles, 2 red marbles, 1 blue marble, and 2 yellow marbles. What is the probability that Helga picks a red marble?
In how many different orders can Latoya, Thomas, and Catherine stand in line at the movie theater?	You toss a penny and roll a die at the same time. What is the probability that the coin will land on heads and the die will land on a 4?	Ben was so hungry that he bought an Italian hero, potato chips, a slice of pizza, and a cinnamon bun. In how many different orders can Ben eat these foods?
Jordan went to the bakery to buy a cake. He could choose either chocolate or vanilla cake. There were four kinds of frosting: fudge, strawberry, cherry, and vanilla. How many different combinations are possible if Jordan must choose one cake flavor and one frosting flavor?	In a bag there are 3 green marbles, 2 red marbles, 2 blue marbles, and 5 yellow marbles. What is the probability that Tyrell picks a green marble, puts it back, then picks a yellow marble?	Michael had 10 books to read for his summer reading. He chose 3 of the 10 books to take to camp with him. How many groups of 3 are possible?

Name(s): _____

These Angles Add Up!

Solve three angle problems
to get Tic-Tac-Math!

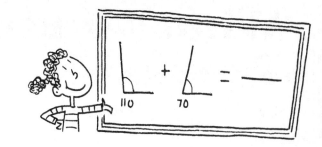

Angles ABC and CBD are supplementary. Angle CBD is 150°. What is the measure of angle ABC?

Angles ABC and CBD are complementary. Angle ABC is 25°. What is the measure of angle CBD?

Angles ABC and CBD are supplementary. Angle CBD is 90°. What is the measure of angle ABC?

Angles ABC and CBD are supplementary. Angle CBD is 104° more than angle ABC. Find the measure of each angle.

Angles ABC and CBD are complementary. Angle CBD is 9 times angle ABC. Find the measure of each angle.

Angles ABC and CBD are complementary. Angle CBD is 4 times the measure of angle ABC. Find the measure of each angle.

Angles ABC and CBD are supplementary. Angle CBD is 6° more than twice the measure of angle ABC. Find the measure of each angle.

Angles ABC and CBD are complementary. Angle CBD is 15° more than twice the measure of angle ABC. Find the measure of each angle.

Angles ABC and CBD are complementary. Angle CBD is 9° more than half of angle ABC. Find the measure of each angle.

Name(s): _____

What "Acute" Triangle!

Solve three problems to get Tic-Tac-Math!

Classify this triangle by its angles:

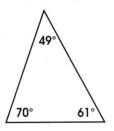

Classify this triangle by its angles:

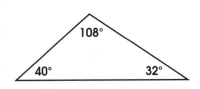

Classify this triangle by the lengths of its sides:

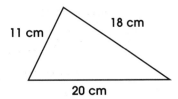

Classify this triangle by its angles and by the lengths of its sides:

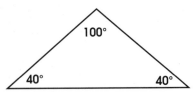

Classify this triangle by the lengths of its sides:

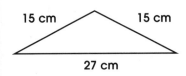

Classify this triangle by its angles and by the lengths of its sides:

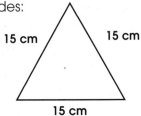

The sum of a triangle's sides is 34.5 cm. The shortest side is 7.5 cm and the middle-length side is 3 cm longer than the shortest side. Find the length of the third side and classify this triangle by the lengths of its sides.

A triangle's longest side is 9 cm. Its shortest side is 5 cm less than that. The third side is 3 cm more than the shortest side. What are the two other lengths of the triangle? How would you classify the triangle by the lengths of its sides?

A triangle's largest angle measure is 3 times that of its smallest angle. The third angle is twice the smallest angle. Classify this triangle by the size of its angles.

Name(s): _____

Classified Quadrilaterals

Solve three problems to get Tic-Tac-Math!

Name this polygon: 	Name this polygon: 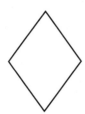	Name this polygon: 
Name this polygon: 	Name this polygon: 	What is another name for a regular quadrilateral?
A figure has two pairs of parallel sides. The top and bottom are equal, and the two sides are equal but different from the top and bottom. All of the angle measures are the same. What is this figure called?	What would you call a rhombus that has four right angles?	A four-sided figure has two acute and two obtuse angles. Two sides are 18 cm long and two sides are 27 cm long. What is the name for this polygon?

Name(s): _____

Geome-tricks!

Use some math magic to solve three perimeter and area problems and get Tic-Tac-Math!

The length of one side of a regular pentagon is 12.5 cm. What is its perimeter?	A rectangle's length is 12.4 cm and its width is 4.9 cm. What is its area?	Find the perimeter of a trapezoid with top base of $2\frac{4}{5}$ inches, bottom base of $5\frac{3}{5}$ inches, and side lengths of $7\frac{3}{5}$ inches and $4\frac{1}{5}$ inches. Write your answer in simplest form.
A triangle's height is 12 inches. Its area is 21 inches. What is the length of its base?	Find the perimeter of a rectangle with length of $9\frac{3}{4}$ inches and width of $3\frac{3}{5}$ inches. Write your answer in simplest form.	The perimeter of a regular octagon is $22\frac{2}{3}$ inches. What is the length of each side?
The length of a side of a regular hexagon is 32.5 cm. What is its perimeter?	The area of a square is 25 square inches. What amount would be $\frac{1}{4}$ of the area? What amount would be $\frac{3}{2}$ of the square's area?	Find the perimeter of a triangle with side lengths $7\frac{3}{4}$ inches, $12\frac{2}{3}$ inches, and $3\frac{1}{8}$ inches. Write your answer in simplest form.

Name(s): _____

Make Room for Volume!

Volume is the amount of space inside a shape.
Solve three volume problems to get Tic-Tac-Math!

A box is 16 cm long, 10 cm wide, and 19 cm high. What is its volume?	The length of the base of a rectangular prism is 12 cm. The height of the prism is 15 cm. If the volume is 1,080 cubic cm, what is the width of the prism's base?	A cube is 19.3 cm on each side. What is its volume?
Find the volume of a cylinder whose height is 19 cm and whose diameter is 14 cm. Use 3.14 as an estimate of pi.	What is the volume of a cylinder whose radius is 4.2 cm and whose height is 20 cm? Use 3.14 as an estimate of pi.	The area of the base of a cylinder is 25.7 square cm. Its height is 12.3 cm. What is its volume?
The volume of a cube is 216 cubic cm. What is the length of each side?	A cardboard box has a volume of 2,058 cubic cm. Its length is 3 times its width. Its height is twice its width. Find the dimensions.	The volume of a cube is 512 cubic cm. What is the length of one of its sides?

Name(s): _____

Are You a Geometry Genius?

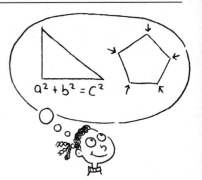

Show off your geometry knowledge by solving three problems to get Tic-Tac-Math!

The legs of a right triangle are 3 cm and 4 cm. Its hypotenuse is 5 cm. What is the area of the triangle?	How many sides does a polygon have if the sum of its angles is 720 degrees?	If a rectangle's area is 3,000 square feet and its width is 40 feet, what is its perimeter?
A photograph of a pink Gerber daisy is 12 cm by 18 cm. If it is proportionally enlarged so that it has four times the area of the original picture, what would be the new dimensions?	A square is folded in half and the crease separates two equivalent rectangles. Each rectangle has a perimeter of 24 inches. What are the dimensions and area of the square?	Farmer Felix has 36 meters of fencing to make a rectangular pen for his cow Miss Bessie. What dimensions would give Miss Bessie the largest area? What would that area be?
A rectangular room has an area of 240 square feet. The length of the room is 8 feet greater than its width. What are the length and width of the room?	One angle of a triangle is 3 times the measure of the second angle. The third angle is twice the measure of the first angle. What are the measures of each angle? Write an equation to solve or use guess-and-check.	A rectangle's length is 3 times its width. Its area is 108 square cm. What are its dimensions?

Scholastic • *Tic-Tac-Math: Grades 5 & Up*

Name(s): _____

Conquer the Clock!

How are you at keeping track of time? Solve three time problems to get Tic-Tac-Math!

How many hours are there in 4 days?	How many minutes are there in 5 hours?	How many seconds are there in 12 minutes?
How many minutes are there in one week?	If your heart beats 72 times a minute, how many times will it beat in one day?	Tanya played basketball for 1 hour and 45 minutes on Tuesday, 2 hours and 20 minutes on Thursday, and 1 hour and 50 minutes on Friday. How much time did she play basketball on those three days altogether?
Matilda set aside 4 hours and 30 minutes to do her statistics project. However, it only took her 2 hours and 55 minutes. How much "extra" time did Matilda have?	Francois ran 1 hour and 45 minutes on Monday, 1 hour and 35 minutes on Wednesday, and 1 hour and 55 minutes on Friday. How much time did he run altogether?	Angel worked 6 hours and 45 minutes on Monday; 8 hours and 50 minutes on Tuesday; 7 hours and 45 minutes on Wednesday; and 6 hours and 35 minutes on Friday. How much time did Angel work altogether?

Scholastic • Tic-Tac-Math: Grades 5 & Up

Name(s): _____

Mix and Match These Skills

Show off your skills by solving three problems to get Tic-Tac-Math!

If you have 3 pairs of pants, 4 sweaters, and 5 shirts, how many days can you wear an outfit consisting of a pair of pants, a sweater, and a shirt before you wear the same outfit again? (Assume all the outfits match!)	Find 701 – 297.	What is the least common multiple of 3, 11, and 9?
Simplify: $$2^3 =$$	What is the value of 1 to the 85th power?	If the diameter of a circle is 24 mm, how long would its radius be?
Which one of the following has at least two congruent bases? a) a cube b) a triangular pyramid c) a pentagon d) a hexagonal pyramid	Write five thousandths in decimal form.	What is the volume of a rectangular prism with a height of 25 cm, a width of 8.3 cm, and a length of 10 cm?

Name(s): _____

The Daily Review

Brush up on various skills by solving three problems to get Tic-Tac-Math!

A ball is dropped from 40 feet and hits the ground. At each bounce it bounces one half the height of its previous bounce. The ball is caught when its bounce is 5 feet high. What is the total distance that the ball has traveled? Make a sketch of the ball's path to help you.	Spencer planted an 18-inch-tall apple tree in his backyard. If the tree grows 5 inches each year, how tall will it be after 7 years?	Hannah ate 50 of the 275 N&N's candies from a big bag. What percent of the bag did she consume? (Round your answer to the nearest whole number.)
Alec was curious about how many calories there were in the whole bottle of Latorade that he had just downed. The label said there were 130 calories in each serving and that the bottle had 2.5 servings. How many calories did Alec drink?	The regular price of a Hermes saddle is $750. Dover Saddlery is having a 30% off sale on all items. What would be the sale price of the Hermes saddle?	What percent of 24 is 8? Round your answer to the nearest whole percent.
1 is what percent of 200?	60 is 20% of what number?	The following are a list of babies' weights: 7.8 lbs, 5.0 lbs, 6.7 lbs, 8.1 lbs, 6.6 lbs, and 9.4 lbs. Find the weight range and the median weight.

Scholastic • Tic-Tac-Math: Grades 5 & Up

Name(s): _____

Mix It Up, DJ!

Check out the sounds of these awesome skills.
Solve three problems to get Tic-Tac-Math!

How much greater is $7\frac{1}{8}$ than $2\frac{3}{5}$?	Rewrite in standard form: 1.356×10^{-4}	Rewrite in scientific notation: 0.00000000003
Rewrite in scientific notation: 785,000,000	Harvey read 6 of the 7 books he took with him to camp. What percent of the books did he read? Round to the nearest whole number.	Ella earned A's on 11 of the 16 math tests she took last year. What percent of her tests were A's? Round your answer to the nearest whole number.
A rectangle's width is p cm. Its length is triple the width. Its perimeter is 72 cm. Find the length and width of the rectangle.	A rectangle's width is w cm. The length is 2 cm less than 8 times the width. The perimeter is 50 cm. Find the length and width of the rectangle.	Poor Jonah. He couldn't remember the combination for his lock. He knew that the three numbers were 18, 30, and 5, but he couldn't remember the order. List all of the possible arrangements for the combination.

Name(s): _____

Four-Star Review

Help yourself to a hearty serving of review problems!
Solve three in a row to get Tic-Tac-Math!

Write the prime factorization of the numbers below. 64 50	Find the greatest common factor (GCF) of each pair of numbers. 12, 18 17, 51	Find the least common multiple (LCM) for the pair of numbers: 24, 16
Find the sum and write in simplest form. $\frac{3}{10} + \frac{17}{10} =$	Solve the equation for x. $x - \frac{3}{5} = \frac{9}{5}$	Four friends buy 36 cookies for $12. Tom gave $2, Jake gave $3, Ted gave $4, and Sam gave $3. Each person gets the number of cookies proportional to the money paid. How many cookies does each person get?
You have a purple polka-dotted fence around your rectangular garden. Its length is 1.5 meters and its width is 0.5 meters. If you put posts around the perimeter at 0.1-meter intervals, how many posts will you need?	What is the sum of the first 20 even numbers?	What is the sum of 6.7 and 2.36?

Scholastic • Tic-Tac-Math: Grades 5 & Up

Name(s): _____

Rev Up
for Review!

Start your engines! The last review activity is underway.
Solve three problems to get Tic-Tac-Math!

$5.2 - 1.75 =$

Juan is making sandwiches for a party. Each sandwich has one type of bread, one type of cheese, and one type of meat. There are two choices each for bread, for cheese, and for meat. How many different sandwiches can Juan make?

Complementary angles are
a) two angles whose sum is a multiple of 10.
b) two angles whose sum is 180 degrees.
c) two angles whose sum is 90 degrees.
d) two angles whose sum is between 90 and 180 degrees.

Write 50.6 in words.

Write fourteen hundredths in decimal form.

$3\frac{1}{2} \times \frac{1}{5} =$

Write the ratio of the number of prime numbers between 10 and 25 to the number of composite numbers between 10 and 25.

Frankie bought 15 pounds of chocolate and put 0.5 pounds in each bag. How many bags of chocolate did Frankie have?

Which of these choices contains the dimensions of a rectangle with the same perimeter as a rectangle with dimensions 5 m by 3 m?
  a) 10 m by 8 m
  b) 7 m by 1 m
  c) 6 m by 4 m
  d) 8 m by 2 m

Scholastic • *Tic-Tac-Math: Grades 5 & Up*

Answers

Let's Have "Sum" Fun!
(p. 9)

10,801	22,416	76,120
762,184	155,181	4,608,022
46,561 waves	160,318 visitors	2,108 pages

Oh, What's the Difference?
(p. 10)

767	1,157	28,962
$112	458 cupcakes	279 miles
113 freckles	16,959 more chocolate chips	88,267 candies

Master Multiplication!
(p. 11)

1,530	1,581	585
28,836 pears	$10,116	15,048 cheetah pox
11,477 wishes	4,380 miles	21,331 screams

Dive Into Division!
(p. 12)

30	302	207
235 R22	1,476 R8	25 miles
97 pepperoni pizzas	29 candies, 15 left over	7 full rows, 4 students partially filling another row

Divisibility Rules Rule!
(p. 13)

3, 5	3, 9	2, 5, 10
4	15	0, 3, or 6
120	44	29

The Factor Factory
(p. 14)

1, 2, 4, 8	1, 2, 7, 14	1, 2, 3, 5, 6, 10, 15, 30
7, 29	37, 41, 47, 53	71, 73, 79, 83, 89, 97
4	9	15

Mad About Multiples!
(p. 15)

20, 30, 35	18, 24, 30	78, 102
28	24	105
In 15 seconds	In 8 seconds	90 inches from the starting line

Deci-mental Powers
(p. 16)

0.48	two and seventy-three hundredths	58.379
5.408	10.172	20 + 6 + 0.7 + 0.03 + 0.001
0.16	0.683	6.4 and 0.1

Order in the Court!
(p. 17)

<	<	>
7.29, 7.284, 7.281	0.5089, 0.509, 0.5092, 0.513	b
9.00 seconds, 10.29 seconds, 10.5 seconds, 10.89 seconds, 11.2 seconds	a	0.0055

"Sum" More Decimals
(p. 18)

6.8	10.45	65.39
84.6 cm	198.3 cm	380.7 cm
390 pounds	$101.38	95.5 mph

Decimal Deli
(p. 19)

3.35	6.85	62.456
1.5 pounds	0.905 pounds	1.728 pounds
7.928 pounds more	0.0177 pounds more	4.3003 pounds

It's Time(s) for Decimals!
(p. 20)

44.5	0.245	2.976
$62.82	79.8 inches	62.08 minutes
$199.20	$85.41	$29.89

Dare to Divide Decimals!
(p. 21)

1.9	1.96	23
2.15	27.375	$.28
4.8 miles per day	42 quarters	66 bags

Make Sense of Cents!
(p. 22)

$1.68	$4.00	1 dime, 12 nickels, and 2 pennies
11 of the coins are quarters	5 coins (3 quarters, 1 dime, and 1 nickel)	• 1 quarter, 3 pennies • 2 dimes, 1 nickel, 3 pennies • 2 dimes, 8 pennies • 1 dime, 3 nickels, 3 pennies • 1 dime, 2 nickels, 8 pennies • 1 dime, 1 nickel, 13 pennies • 1 dime, 18 pennies • 5 nickels, 3 pennies • 4 nickels, 8 pennies • 3 nickels, 13 pennies • 2 nickels, 18 pennies • 1 nickel, 23 pennies • 28 pennies
$1,309; they will need 5 buses because 4 buses will only hold 176 people	$30	6 hours

Fractions Beyond Compare
(p. 23)

$\frac{10}{18}, \frac{3}{4}, \frac{15}{28}, \frac{9}{16}$	$\frac{1}{7}, \frac{6}{18}$	$\frac{10}{20}, \frac{22}{44}, \frac{36}{72}$
$\frac{2}{3}$ of a pizza	Marco	They both swam an equal distance.
Bekah	Paula Sue	Pascal

Add "Sum" Fractions!
(p. 24)

$\frac{5}{6}$	$3\frac{5}{8}$	$\frac{7}{9}$
$1\frac{7}{12}$	$11\frac{11}{40}$	$15\frac{7}{8}$
$\frac{5}{8}$ of the pan	$50\frac{3}{8}$ inches	$17\frac{23}{24}$ miles

Fraction Leftovers
(p. 25)

$\frac{1}{2}$	$4\frac{2}{5}$	$\frac{11}{16}$
$5\frac{3}{10}$	$6\frac{1}{4}$	$5\frac{1}{4}$ pounds
$3\frac{2}{5}$ pans	$1\frac{3}{8}$ "	$6\frac{9}{20}$ miles

Recipe for Multipli-Fractions
(p. 26)

$1\frac{1}{8}$	$\frac{4}{15}$	$\frac{5}{11}$
$22\frac{1}{5}$	21	$8\frac{7}{16}$
$2\frac{1}{4}$ cups	$\frac{1}{2}$ mile	$10\frac{2}{7}$ " tall

I Will Divide This Fraction in Half!
(p. 27)

30	16	$\frac{5}{6}$
20	$7\frac{1}{2}$	9
16 strips	$\frac{1}{16}$ pound	11 bags with $\frac{1}{4}$ pound left over

Ratio Rodeo
(p. 28)

$\frac{1}{2}$	$\frac{2}{3}$	$\frac{1}{2}$
$y = 120$	$x = 60$	$x = 30$
$2\frac{1}{4}$ cups oil	$\frac{1}{2}''$ by $\frac{7}{8}''$	$x = 96$ toy cars

Percent Scents?
(p. 29)

8	132	64 right and 16 wrong
162	49	195 girls
87.4	$18.25	$25.20

Percent Power!
(p. 30)

24%	84%	5%
25%	88%	31%
23%	43%	16%

Donut Wholes
(p. 31)

70	320	16 math tests
60 cookies	550	25 presents
75 jelly beans	50 students	$2,160

We're All Equal!
(p. 32)

0.25	$\frac{3}{5}$	70%
$\frac{5}{8}$	0.1	$\frac{2}{5}$
9.8%, 24%, $\frac{7}{20}$, $\frac{3}{8}$, 0.38, 0.52	0.74, 0.6, $\frac{1}{2}$, 0.48, 47.5%, $\frac{3}{10}$	0.05, $\frac{1}{10}$, $\frac{1}{5}$, 25%, $\frac{1}{3}$, 0.35, 45%, 0.55

Super Powers
(p. 33)

64	27	1,024
0.0001	0.025	7×10^{-3}
3.08×10^{-2}	7,530	500.2008

Absolutely Positive!
(p. 34)

8	13	<
>	+10	+4
−18	She added −8 instead of +8. Her answer should have been −1.	+20

Meet Patty Pattern!
(p. 35)

35, 40, 45 (add 5 to the previous number)	44, 53, 62 (add 9 to the previous number)	62, 59, 56 (subtract 3 from the previous number)
6, 7, 2 (subtract 5 from the previous number, then add 1 to the difference)	4, 2, −1 (subtract 3 from the previous number, then subtract 2 from the difference)	48, 96, 192 (multiply the previous number by 2)
64, 32, 16 (divide the previous number by 2)	−3, 0, 3 (add 3 to the previous number)	−18, −19, −9 (add 10 to the previous number, subtract 2 from the sum, subtract 1 from the difference)

Three Cheers for Decimal Patterns! (p. 36)

5.4, 5.5, 5.6 (add 0.1 to the previous number)	10.45, 10.35, 10.25 (subtract 0.1 from the previous number)	7.9, 7.6, 7.3 (subtract 0.3 from the previous number)
31, 38.7, 46.4 (add 7.7 to the previous number)	0.28, 0.3, 0.32 (add 0.02 to the previous number)	0.1, 0.11, 0.12 (add 0.01 to the previous number)
0.0005, 0.00005, 0.000005 (divide the previous number by 10 or multiply it by 0.1)	5.4, 16.2, 48.6 (multiply the previous number by 3)	6.45, 5.85, 5.25 (subtract 0.6 from the previous number)

I Detect a Pattern (p. 37)

$\frac{9}{8}, \frac{11}{8}, \frac{13}{8}$ (add $\frac{1}{4}$ or $\frac{2}{8}$ to the previous number)	$\frac{13}{3}, \frac{16}{3}, \frac{19}{3}$ (add 1 or $\frac{3}{3}$ to the previous number)	$\frac{1}{64}, \frac{1}{128}, \frac{1}{256}$ (divide the previous number by 2 or multiply it by $\frac{1}{2}$)
$\frac{3}{112}, \frac{3}{224}, \frac{3}{448}$ (divide the previous number by 2 or multiply it by $\frac{1}{2}$)	$1\frac{1}{2}, 1\frac{1}{4}, 1$ (subtract $\frac{1}{4}$ from the previous number)	$\frac{4}{5}, 1\frac{2}{5}, 1$ (add $\frac{3}{5}$ to the previous number; then subtract $\frac{2}{5}$ from that number)
$1\frac{4}{5}, 2, 1\frac{3}{5}$ (subtract $\frac{2}{5}$ from the previous number; then add $\frac{1}{5}$ to that number)	$3\frac{7}{8}, 4\frac{1}{8}, 4$ (add $\frac{1}{4}$ to the previous number; then subtract $\frac{1}{8}$ from that number)	$10\frac{2}{3}, 21\frac{1}{3}, 42\frac{2}{3}$ (multiply the previous number by 2)

Pass the Pattern Table! (p. 38)

14, 8, 9 (A + 3 = B)	5, 9, 13 (A − 5 = B)	70, 30, 30 (A x 10 = B)
17, 10, 2.5 (A + 2 = B)	9, −10 (A x 3 = B)	$2\frac{1}{4}, \frac{5}{8}, \frac{11}{8}$ (A + $\frac{1}{4}$ = B)
29, 2 ((A x 3) − 1 = B)	21, −2 ((A x 2) + 1 = B)	−7, 2.5 (2A − 3 = B)

x Marks the Spot! (p. 39)

15	12	6
11	9	37
2	h = 2s + $1.27; $3.25	s = 3c − $.88; $3.29

Simplifying Sampler (p. 40)

$\frac{1}{3}$	$\frac{1}{2}$	1
$\frac{1}{3}$	$\frac{1}{4}$	$\frac{1}{4}$
$\frac{10}{11}$	$\frac{8}{29}$	$\frac{1}{10}$

FraXions (p. 41)

$x = 4$	$x = 2$	$x = 4$
$x = 2$	$x = 8$	$\frac{24}{40}$
$\frac{9}{12}$	1	$\frac{4}{13}$

Give y a Try! (p. 42)

y + y + 5 + 5 = 34 cm; y = 12 cm	y + y + 2 + 2 = 10; y = 3 cm	H + 3H = 60; Harold is 15 years old and his father is 45
F + F + 5 = 27; Francisco is 11 and Oriana is 16	3B − B = 8; Bella is 4, Ella is 8, and Stella is 12	4H + 3 − H = 30; Harlan is 9 and his dad is 39
N + 2N + 2N − 3 = 32; Natasha has 7 ribbons, Sally has 14, and Bethany has 11	P + 3P + 3P − 6 = 36; 6 plain, 18 honey-dipped, and 12 chocolate frosted	T + T + 2 + 2T + 4 = 42; Ty made 9 baskets, Malcolm made 11, and Fred made 22

Try Using a Table! (p. 43)

2 quarters, 2 dimes, 2 nickels, and 1 penny	10 $10 tickets and 15 $4 tickets	17 Gooberlings and 22 Farfalles
8 five-petaled flowers and 12 seven-petaled flowers	17 nickels and 28 dimes	14 dimes and 7 quarters
1 quarter, 4 dimes, and 7 nickels	5 pennies, 4 nickels, and 9 dimes	4 triangles, 2 squares, and 2 hexagons

Mean and Median à la Mode (p. 44)

6.5 or $6\frac{1}{2}$	median: 3; mode: 3; range: 6	mean: 3.2; median: 3; mode: 1; range: 5
16	3	7
10	30	18

Above-Average Kids
(p. 45)

mean: 4; median: 3.5	mean: $84	mean: 42; median: 44
mean: 79; median: 80. Choose the median score.	48	mean: 11; median: 7
median: 18; range: 17; mode: 17	mean: 38; median: 33	mean: 8; median: 7; mode: 5; range: 17

What's Your Probability Ability?
(p. 46)

$\frac{1}{2}$	$\frac{1}{3}$	$\frac{1}{6}$
6 different orders	$\frac{1}{12}$	24 different orders
8 combinations	$\frac{5}{48}$	120 groups of 3

These Angles Add Up!
(p. 47)

30°	65°	90°
angle ABC = 38° and angle CBD = 142°	angle ABC = 9° and angle CBD = 81°	angle ABC = 18° and angle CBD = 72°
angle ABC = 58° and angle CBD = 122°	angle ABC = 25° and angle CBD = 65°	angle ABC = 54° and angle CBD = 36°

What "Acute" Triangle!
(p. 48)

acute triangle	obtuse triangle	scalene triangle
obtuse isosceles triangle	isosceles triangle	acute equilateral triangle
16.5 cm; scalene triangle	4 cm and 7 cm; scalene triangle	30°, 60°, and 90°; right triangle

Classified Quadrilaterals
(p. 49)

parallelogram	rhombus	trapezoid
quadrilateral	isosceles trapezoid	square
rectangle	square	parallelogram

Geome-tricks!
(p. 50)

62.5 cm	60.76 cm	$20\frac{1}{5}$ "
3.5"	$26\frac{7}{10}$ "	$2\frac{5}{6}$ "
195 cm	$6\frac{1}{4}$ sq. in. ; $37\frac{1}{2}$ sq. in.	$23\frac{13}{24}$ "

Make Room for Volume!
(p. 51)

3,040 cubic cm	6 cm	7,189.057 cubic cm
2,923.34 cubic cm	1,107.792 cubic cm	316.11 cubic cm

6 cm	width = 7 cm;
	length = 21 cm;
	height = 14 cm
		8 cm

Are You a Geometry Genius?
(p. 52)

6 sq. cm	6 sides	230 feet (its dimensions are 40 feet by 75 feet)
24 cm by 36 cm	8 inches by 8 inches; area = 64 square inches	9 feet by 9 feet; area = 81 square feet
length = 20 feet; width = 12 feet	x + 3x + 6x = 180; 18°, 54°, and 108°	length = 18 cm; width = 6 cm

Conquer the Clock!
(p. 53)

96 hours	300 minutes	720 seconds
10,080 minutes	103,680 times	5 hours and 55 minutes
1 hour and 35 minutes	5 hours and 15 minutes	29 hours and 55 minutes

Mix and Match These Skills
(p. 54)

60 days	404	99
8	1	12 mm
a	0.005	2,075 cubic cm

The Daily Review
(p. 55)

105 feet	53 inches	18%
325 calories	$525	33%
0.5%	300	range = 4.4 lbs; median = 7.25

Mix It Up, DJ!
(p. 56)

$4\frac{21}{40}$	0.0001356	3×10^{-11}
7.85×10^{8}	86%	69%
width = 9 cm; length = 27 cm	width = 3 cm; length = 22 cm	{18, 30, 5}, {18, 5, 30}, {30, 18, 5}, {30, 5, 18}, {5, 18, 30}, {5, 30, 18}

Four-Star Review
(p. 57)

$64 = 2 \times 2 \times 2 \times 2 \times 2 \times 2$; $50 = 2 \times 5 \times 5$	12, 18: 6; 17, 51: 17	48
2	$\frac{12}{5}$	Tom gets 6 cookies, Jake gets 9, Ted gets 12, and Sam gets 9
40 posts	420	9.06

Rev Up for Review!
(p. 58)

3.45	8 different sandwiches	c
fifty and six tenths	0.14	$\frac{7}{10}$
$\frac{5}{9}$	30 bags	b